Unbound

A DEVOTIONAL FOR MEN IN PURSUIT
OF A LIFE WITH JESUS

PAPER PEONY PRESS

UNBOUND: A DEVOTIONAL FOR MEN
© Paper Peony Press.
First Edition, 2022

Published by: Paper Peony Press
www.paperpeonypress.com

For wholesale inquiries contact: reagan@paperpeonypress.com

Printed in China

ISBN - 978-1-952842-86-3

this journal belongs to:

_____

_____

_____

DEDICATION

To Mom, Sophia, Skye, Sevyn, and my band of brothers, "The Magnificent 7" (Wayne, Erick, Dale, Nate, Johnny, Hank, and Tony).

INTRODUCTION

The most transformative experiences in my walk with God have occurred in two ways consistently. One, when I devote meaningful time in God's Word with the intention for application. And two, sharing God's Word in community with a small group.

I hope that this devotional serves you in both ways, bringing you together intentionally around the Word of God.

You can expect an underlining of God's glory revealed and a charge to release our expectations of how He is supposed to operate in our life.

I thank God for the opportunity to support you in this way, and I'm incredibly grateful for the team at Paper Peony Press for the encouragement on this journey.

Let's dive in...

 **Unbound**

DAY 01

"Look!" Nebuchadnezzar shouted. "I see four men, unbound, walking around in the fire unharmed! And the fourth looks like a god!"

Daniel 3:25 NLT

Speaking to many nonbelievers or even those considering the acceptance of Christ as their Savior, one familiar "sentiment" is sure to surface—the limitations that they believe will come after choosing to follow Jesus.

This passage delivers a most crushing blow to that fallacy, the false notion that when we follow Christ our world becomes limited. Nebuchadnezzar, the most powerful person in their known world at this time, who was absolutely furious moments ago, now not only watches in amazement, he's also praising the Most High God, our God.

If you're straddling the fence, this is a call for you to go all in with Jesus Christ. Following Jesus unbounds us from the limitations of this world. It removes us from a finite world of capabilities and places us in an infinite world of possibilities. We are not capable of the thoughts and ways of God, which means we cannot even begin to imagine the strategies God is capable of using to solve our earthly problems.

READ

Grab your bible and look up the scripture to read the surrounding text.

EXAMINE

What is happening in this text?
What does it teach me about God?

APPLY

What does this mean for my life?

PRAY

 # But First, Wait

DAY 02

"I waited patiently for the LORD to help me, and he turned to me and heard my cry. He lifted me out of the pit of despair, out of the mud and the mire. He set my feet on solid ground and steadied me as I walked along."

Psalm 40:1-2 NLT

Most of us have never been stuck in a pit or in sinking sands like we've witnessed many times during a movie. But perhaps your vehicle has been caught in the mud or you've been stranded by the side of the highway with a flat tire.

Can you recall the immediate thought of "what now?" and how you automatically shifted into the protocols you've been taught?

Waiting is typically not the first nor is it the most exciting choice. It can be a scary feeling to relinquish control. However, there are a significant number of times when God has called His people to wait in order to unlock wisdom and greater power, and ultimately to reveal His glory.

Abraham was told to wait; Moses was made to wait; Joseph waited; and Jesus's last instruction to His followers before His ascension was to wait for the Holy Spirit before they could go out and forever change the world.

Waiting goes against our daily conditioning, but it is a foundational principle in the kingdom of God. It unlocks solutions and wisdom way beyond our imagination. God's thoughts are higher than our thoughts as far as the heavens separate the earth. You can imagine Moses felt a hint of this when the sea parted before him. Joseph must have too when he reflected on being second in command only to Pharaoh after being tossed into a pit without knowing what would come next.

Wouldn't you rather have God's solution than your best idea? Take some time to reflect on the times He revealed His glory and made a way for you with solutions that would never have crossed your mind.

READ

Grab your bible and look up the scripture to read the surrounding text.

EXAMINE

What is happening in this text?
What does it teach me about God?

APPLY

What does this mean for my life?

PRAY

📖 Activate Your Faith

DAY 03

"I also said to the king, "If it please the king, let me have letters addressed to the governors of the province west of the Euphrates River, instructing them to let me travel safely through their territories on my way to Judah..." And the king granted these requests, because the gracious hand of God was on me."

Nehemiah 2:7-8 NLT

Throughout the book of Nehemiah, we find an outline of how we should activate our calling and the desires God has placed on our hearts. From start to finish, Nehemiah displays an example we should all follow.

Notice his acknowledgment that God's hand was on him. Starting something can be hard and scary. Many of us aren't able to acknowledge God's favor in most situations simply because we won't even take the first step.

How will we know if the favor of God is on us if we won't move on the things we've prayed to Him about? We paralyze ourselves with doubt, finding every reasonable and logical response to deter us from moving in faith.

Everything worth doing will require us to jump mental and spiritual hurdles. In verse 2 of this passage, Nehemiah actually expresses something prior to acknowledging God's favor on him. He writes of how dreadfully afraid he came to the king to state his request. Fear is often present, so instead of a paralyzer, let it be a reminder to activate our faith in the God who holds all power.

READ
Grab your bible and look up the scripture to read the surrounding text.

EXAMINE
What is happening in this text?
What does it teach me about God?

APPLY
What does this mean for my life?

PRAY

📖 We've Been Equipped

DAY 04

"For God has not given us a spirit of fear, but of power and of love and of a sound mind."

2 Timothy 1:7 NKJV

"So I'm happy tonight. I'm not worried about anything. I'm not fearing any man. Mine eyes have seen the glory of the coming of the Lord!"

These are words from Martin Luther King Jr's speech, "I've Been to the Mountaintop," given just a day before his assassination.

Twenty-five thousand individuals had gathered once more to see MLK advocate on behalf of their rights. With his gift stirred up, he stood in solidarity with the poor and the hurting in order to help them find their voice, even if it meant losing his own life.

We may look at instances like this and wonder how it was possible for the people of God to stand in such boldness. We can typically find that answer by understanding what Jesus left for us.

Jesus's ascension made it possible for the Spirit of the Lord to dwell within us. Because of this, we're equipped with power, love, and a sound mind to activate the gifts within us. More than ever, the world needs boldness from the people of God, to witness and to stand in the midst of fear and uncertainty. For us to do this, we must invite the Spirit of God.

When you feel paralyzed by fear, ask the Holy Spirit to fill you and empower you to carry out the work God has for you.

READ
Grab your bible and look up the scripture to read the surrounding text.

EXAMINE
What is happening in this text?
What does it teach me about God?

APPLY
What does this mean for my life?

PRAY

📖 Remain in Obedience

DAY 05

"And Pharaoh said unto his servants, Can we find such a one as this is, a man in whom the Spirit of God is? And Pharaoh said unto Joseph, Forasmuch as God hath shewed thee all this, there is none so discreet and wise as thou art: Thou shalt be over my house, and according unto thy word shall all my people be ruled: only in the throne will I be greater than thou. And Pharaoh said unto Joseph, See, I have set thee over all the land of Egypt."

Genesis 41:38-41 KJV

You can easily find people who consider the Old Testament to be unrelatable. It can certainly feel unrelatable at times, considering the various practices and ceremonies.

However, though our practices may have changed over time, God's practice to honor obedience is the same today as it was then—and that is something for us to take comfort in.

To know that, no matter where you begin, you can be accompanied by God's favor and presence through your obedience to His Word is a stronghold in this world of uncertainty.

It's also important to understand that when you've received the favor of God and have been elevated to more, the expectation is to remain in God's presence through obeying His Word.

If we're not careful, promotion and recognition can create separation from the One who has elevated us there in the first place. This separation begins when we abandon humility and forget to glorify the One who is establishing our path.

Honor God's faithfulness wherever you are today by standing in obedience to God and His statutes.

READ

Grab your bible and look up the scripture to read the surrounding text.

EXAMINE

What is happening in this text?
What does it teach me about God?

APPLY

What does this mean for my life?

PRAY

Devote
yourselves
to prayer.

Colossians 4:2

Weekly Reflection

📖 Give Room for His Glory

DAY 06

"But Moses told the people, "Don't be afraid. Just stand still and watch the LORD rescue you today. The Egyptians you see today will never be seen again. The LORD himself will fight for you. Just stay calm."

Exodus 14:13-14 NLT

Can you imagine being told to "stay calm" while a locust-like army is fiercely approaching?

The situation is overwhelming, the outlook is completely bleak, and all the odds seem to be in favor of your ultimate defeat. Yet, there is a greater purpose to be revealed in this situation—God's glory.

Life with God is a constant acknowledgment of His glory at work, and the less we interfere, the greater the opportunity for it to be displayed.

Countless times throughout scripture, we are asked to stay calm and trust in the Lord, our stronghold, so that His glory can be revealed in our lives and situations.

It's natural to question "why" when we find ourselves with our back against the wall. But be encouraged by God's faithfulness throughout history. Let His promises to fight for you be the comfort you lean on in times of uncertainty.

READ

Grab your bible and look up the scripture to read the surrounding text.

EXAMINE

What is happening in this text?
What does it teach me about God?

APPLY

What does this mean for my life?

PRAY

📖 He Cannot Deny Himself

DAY 07

"If we are faithless, he remains faithful, for he cannot deny himself. "

2 Timothy 2:13 CSB

Take a moment to think about the most faithful individual you know. Perhaps it's a parent or best friend, a spouse, or even an employee.

You'll likely find yourself thinking carefully, maybe in an attempt to better understand what the word *faithful* means.

An internet search will give you this definition of faithful: "remaining loyal and steadfast." But for the best definition and evidence, read through the book of Judges.

Although encouraging, the book of Judges can be heartbreaking. Even through consistent denial, Judges shows time after time where the Lord was mindful of the cries of His people. Not only did He listen to the cries of His people, but He was also faithful to respond because He cannot deny His faithful character.

One thing we can be certain of is that God hears us when we know Him and call on Him. 1 John 5:14 (NLT) says, "And we are confident that he hears us whenever we ask for anything that pleases him."

In times when you feel hopeless, take some time to reflect on how faithful the Lord has been throughout your life. This type of reflection has the power to strengthen you—and others who need it too.

READ

Grab your bible and look up the scripture to read the surrounding text.

EXAMINE

What is happening in this text?
What does it teach me about God?

APPLY

What does this mean for my life?

PRAY

There's Power in Your Words

DAY 08

**"Return to your own house, and tell what great
things God has done for you."**

Luke 8:39 NKJV

Has Jesus done something wonderful in your life recently?

And have you shared this victory with the people you know?

Our personal testimony is undoubtedly one of the most impactful tools in the kingdom of God. Revelations 12:11 speaks about the power of overcoming through the blood of the Lamb and the word of our testimony.

In other words, people find freedom through what Jesus has already done for us and by telling people what He has done for us.

So, when Jesus says, "Go and tell of what I have done for you," it is not to be taken lightly. It has world-changing power for those who believe.

Your encounters with Jesus become an invitation for others to overcome their own trials through the testimony you choose to share.

How can you help others find freedom today by sharing what God has done for you?

READ
Grab your bible and look up the scripture to read the surrounding text.

EXAMINE
What is happening in this text? What does it teach me about God?

APPLY
What does this mean for my life?

PRAY

 # Walk in Confidence

DAY 09

"But in that coming day no weapon turned against you will succeed. You will silence every voice raised up to accuse you. These benefits are enjoyed by the servants of the LORD; their vindication will come from me. I, the LORD, have spoken!"

Isaiah 54:17 NLT

A common prayer for my wife and I is to present as good ambassadors for the kingdom of heaven. Our hope is to be a great representation in a world that is not ours.

An ambassador is also an appropriate reference given the amount of power and authority we have behind us through our faith in Jesus. It is the same grave-defying authority we all have as Christians.

And though we don't walk around picking fights and waving this authority, we can walk our journey in confidence knowing that the Almighty is on our side even when we feel out of place.

This is just one of the empowering promises of God. Are you taking the time to know the promises for those that belong to the Lord?

READ

Grab your bible and look up the scripture to read the surrounding text.

EXAMINE

What is happening in this text?
What does it teach me about God?

APPLY

What does this mean for my life?

PRAY

God Plus Nothing Equals Everything

DAY 10

"Then the LORD said to Gideon, "The people are still too many; bring them down to the water and I will test them for you there. So it shall be that he of whom I say to you, 'This one shall go with you,' he shall go with you; but everyone of whom I say to you, 'This one shall not go with you,' he shall not go.""

Judges 7:4 NASB

How many times have you thought to yourself, *If only I had enough?* Enough money, time, people, resources. . . you name it.

Often, we tend to equate success or the likelihood of success with more of something.

However, this is the opposite of what we see in scripture. Instead of an abundance,

God looks at the substance. "For the LORD sees not as man sees: man looks on the outward appearance, but the LORD looks on the heart" (1 Samuel 16:7 ESV).

When you feel overwhelmed, inadequate, or lacking in an area, reflect on how perfectly God works in these situations. From beginning to end, the Word of God shows us how He changes the world with the substance of heart rather than an abundance of resources.

When you feel inadequate, consider what God has done for you (and others) when the only thing that you add to the equation is faith.

READ

Grab your bible and look up the scripture to read the surrounding text.

EXAMINE

What is happening in this text?
What does it teach me about God?

APPLY

What does this mean for my life?

PRAY

Stand firm in the faith.

1 Corinthians 16:13

Weekly Reflection

# Win in Every Season

DAY 11

"How much better to get wisdom than gold! To get understanding is to be chosen rather than silver."

Proverbs 16:16 ESV

I believe there are moments and seasons in life when God wants to present a bag full of wealth to us.

Before you begin to spend, consider this: This wealth likely won't come in the form of money. These bags are often situations, moments, and seasons that are bitter and filled with hurt, disappointment, or even grief.

How is this considered wealth? Instead of treasures that can be destroyed or stolen, God often gives us an opportunity to gain wisdom. This wisdom is not only precious, but it compounds at an unmatched rate when you've truly grasped what God is trying to teach you in these times.

For with this wisdom, you'll make righteous decisions and practices that guide the rest of your life and even the lives of your family members, storing up treasures in heaven and making true impact here on earth.

These jackpot moments are given daily; however, the ability to take the winnings depends on our diligence to seek and trust whatever the situation is.

READ

Grab your bible and look up the scripture to read the surrounding text.

EXAMINE

What is happening in this text?
What does it teach me about God?

APPLY

What does this mean for my life?

PRAY

 **It's a Heart Issue**

DAY 12

"The good person out of his good treasure brings forth good, and the evil person out of his evil treasure brings forth evil."

Matthew 12:35 ESV

I was taught by a mentor once about the importance of healthy confrontation.

The word *confrontation* derives from the medieval word *confrontationem*, simply meaning to bring two parties together face-to-face to explore the truth.

As Christians, we can sometimes be very bad at confronting issues for three reasons: One, it's difficult, meaning it often takes time and effort. Two, we take offense, making issues become personal when they shouldn't be. And three, our hearts are not right.

Take, for example, Jesus's confrontation with the accusers of the woman who committed adultery—no doubt a contemptuous opportunity, ultimately resulting in people reflecting and walking away.

Our world could look much different if we as followers of Christ chose not to avoid the issues around us but to engage with a heart full of love and compassion like Jesus did. It takes time and should be very uncomfortable for us—for that means we're growing in our walk to become more like Jesus.

READ

Grab your bible and look up the scripture to read the surrounding text.

EXAMINE

What is happening in this text?
What does it teach me about God?

APPLY

What does this mean for my life?

PRAY

📖 Don't Stray

DAY 13

"Be sober-minded; be watchful. Your adversary the devil prowls around like a roaring lion, seeking someone to devour."

1 Peter 5:8 ESV

I was truly surprised the first time I understood how lions and most predators hunt. For some reason, my thought was that a great beast would boldly jump into any herd and slay the first thing that it saw.

However, too many animal shows with David Attenborough teach how these predators identify, stalk, and devour those they can isolate.

Often when we're low and feeling out, we isolate ourselves from church, community, loved ones, and even the presence of God.

This is a mistake. The enemy preys on our weakness with the objective to destroy us, but in our weakness, we can find strength and cover with God.

Be mindful of the position you take when you feel down. Do you withdraw completely, or do you draw near to God?

READ
Grab your bible and look up the scripture to read the surrounding text.

EXAMINE
What is happening in this text?
What does it teach me about God?

APPLY
What does this mean for my life?

PRAY

📖 Get to Know Your Tools

DAY 14

"Flee from sexual immorality. Every other sin a person commits is outside the body, but the sexually immoral person sins against his own body. Or do you not know that your body is a temple of the Holy Spirit within you, whom you have from God? You are not your own, for you were bought with a price. So glorify God in your body."

1 Corinthians 6:18-20 ESV

As men, it's time for us to recognize that strength comes in many forms. Discipline itself is a form of strength, and many times so is dependency. For followers of Christ, it's the discipline to follow and rely on the tried-and-true principles of God.

Of course, we must be aware of that wisdom in order to apply it. We've been given the playbook on how to be strong in one of the most detrimental struggles in life, sexual immorality.

The play is simple, but the execution takes strength in the form of discipline. Whatever that tempting situation may look like, God gives us assurance that He provides a way out.

The back button on your phone, the keys in your pocket, the words that you need to express—it's all there if we'll take His wisdom and have the strength to flee. You do not have to conform to what is expected in a given situation, you only need to apply His wisdom, and in doing so, you give God the glory.

In what areas today do you need God's wisdom regarding sexual immorality?

READ

Grab your bible and look up the scripture to read the surrounding text.

EXAMINE

What is happening in this text?
What does it teach me about God?

APPLY

What does this mean for my life?

PRAY

📖 What Are You Thinking?

DAY 15

"Finally, brothers and sisters, whatever is true, whatever is noble, whatever is right, whatever is pure, whatever is lovely, whatever is admirable—if anything is excellent or praiseworthy— think about such things."

Philippians 4:8 NIV

Are you thinking about what you're thinking about?

The Greek word for *meditate* means "to ponder, to consider, and cognate."

Not until we take inventory do we realize how often we allow our minds to run uncontrollably to whatever the world puts in front of us.
To meditate on scripture and ways of righteous living is taking ownership of what

God has given us to steward well. When we don't meditate on the truth, we allow the world to steer our path. And though it may feel innocent, the world does not have our best intention in mind.

So, are you thinking about what you're thinking about?

READ

Grab your bible and look up the scripture to read the surrounding text.

EXAMINE

What is happening in this text? What does it teach me about God?

APPLY

What does this mean for my life?

PRAY

For the word of God is alive and active.

Hebrews 4:12

Weekly Reflection

📖 Does It Measure Up?

DAY 16

"All Scripture is inspired by God and is useful to teach us what is true and to make us realize what is wrong in our lives. It corrects us when we are wrong and teaches us to do what is right. God uses it to prepare and equip his people to do every good work."

2 Timothy 3:16-17 NLT

One day while driving, a man pulled up next to me and shouted "Why so sad, man of God?!" I hadn't realized my countenance reflected one of sadness even though I wasn't sad. After realizing he must have seen my "Jesus On Board" sticker on my truck's window, I smiled and let him know I was only deep in thought.

His response, I believe, is a perspective taken by many, "You're not supposed to be sad; Jesus was never sad." This of course isn't true, but he got me thinking about how we learn about Jesus.

There's so much information out there for us today that it can be overwhelming. According to Forbes, every minute there are over six hundred Wikipedia edits. And over the last two years alone, 90% of the data in the world was generated.

You can imagine the vast amount of information out there. However, there is one source that is God-breathed and God-inspired to equip you with understanding the heart of God and who He is. The Word of God not only paints the best picture of our Lord, it helps us to develop a relationship that is personal to each of us.

Are you measuring the information you receive about your life with the Word of God?

READ

Grab your bible and look up the scripture to read the surrounding text.

EXAMINE

What is happening in this text?
What does it teach me about God?

APPLY

What does this mean for my life?

PRAY

📖 Everyday Choices

DAY 17

"But Nineveh has more than 120,000 people living in spiritual darkness, not to mention all the animals. Shouldn't I feel sorry for such a great city?"

Jonah 4:11 NLT

The complexities of life are so broad and diverse. There are a great number of struggles that just one person can experience even in a single day.

With this enormous range of struggles, we can acknowledge that we all would rather receive love from our neighbors rather than conviction, hope over despair, and examples of faith instead of arrogance.

Consider God's response to Jonah in this text. Rather than leaving the people of Nineveh to perish as Jonah believed they should, God used Jonah to deliver a message of reconciliation.

I've heard Pastor Dan Dean say it like this: "Our job is to love, the Holy Spirit's to convict, and God's to judge."

The world is filled with spiritual darkness. By removing our often natural disposition to convict and judge people, we can spread light through our choice to love.

There's no doubt you'll have the option to love or judge today, which will you choose?

READ
Grab your bible and look up the scripture to read the surrounding text.

EXAMINE
What is happening in this text?
What does it teach me about God?

APPLY
What does this mean for my life?

PRAY

📖 He Will Take Care of You

DAY 18

"Give your burdens to the LORD, and he will take care of you. He will not permit the godly to slip and fall."

Psalm 55:22 NLT

Make no mistake, Jesus grants us access.

A pastor friend shared a story of sending a staff member to make purchases on behalf of the church using the church's credit card.

The problem was when this staff member went to make these considerably large purchases, the card was declined. The staff member soon realized that the pastor had accidentally given her his personal card and not the church's.

Many times we're denied in various areas of life because we're seeking to make it all happen on our own capacity and strength.

As children of the one true God, we can rely on His abundant resources to provide for us in all our needs, and the primary requirement for accessing His abundance is trust.

Is there something you're pursuing, but you're relying on your own understanding and strength for it?

READ

Grab your bible and look up the scripture to read the surrounding text.

EXAMINE

What is happening in this text?
What does it teach me about God?

APPLY

What does this mean for my life?

PRAY

📖 Stand Firm in Truth

DAY 19

"Then we will no longer be immature like children. We won't be tossed and blown about by every wind of new teaching. We will not be influenced when people try to trick us with lies so clever they sound like the truth."

Ephesians 4:14 NLT

Did you know that, according to cult expert Steve Eichel, there are an estimated ten thousand cults currently in the US today?

Here's the thing—only outsiders with a negative perspective of that practice will call a group a cult. Those involved would fight to keep their practices from being known that way.

In fact, you can find writings of the Roman governor Pliny the Younger in the year 112 describing the Way/Christianity as a cult because he was baffled by their practices of kindness and their devotion to Jesus.

Time has shown there is only one true God; His Son was sent to save our souls from our sins, and the testimonies of His mercies have changed the lives of countless people across centuries.

The Bible warns us of the ongoing deception that we will face as followers of Christ.

Are you truly following Jesus Christ and not an individual, group, or new teaching?

READ

Grab your bible and look up the scripture to read the surrounding text.

EXAMINE

What is happening in this text?
What does it teach me about God?

APPLY

What does this mean for my life?

PRAY

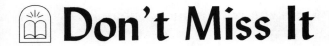# Don't Miss It

DAY 20

"They stood there amazed and perplexed. "What can this mean?" they asked each other. But others in the crowd ridiculed them, saying, "They're just drunk, that's all!""

Acts 2:12-13 NLT

Don't miss it—be sensitive to the move of the Holy Spirit.

The distractions from what God wants to do in your life are endless. Peers, pride, and panic can remove your time to press in with God in an instant.

Here we have an outpouring of God's presence through the Holy Spirit like never before, yet among this great move, there was still doubt and ridicule from people.

This certainly tells us two things: No matter how great the presence of God is in your life, there will always be those that question what you're doing. Secondly, we can miss the work that God is doing around us because it is foreign to us.

Don't miss the work of God around you by closing your heart or putting God in a box for how He is supposed to operate.

Are you expecting God to move based on what you understand?

READ
Grab your bible and look up the scripture to read the surrounding text.

EXAMINE
What is happening in this text?
What does it teach me about God?

APPLY
What does this mean for my life?

PRAY

Act justly, love mercy, walk humbly.

Micah 6:8

Weekly Reflection

📖 Who's the Mediator Here?

DAY 21

"He prayed to the LORD, "Isn't this what I said, LORD, when I was still at home? That is what I tried to forestall by fleeing to Tarshish. I knew that you are a gracious and compassionate God, slow to anger and abounding in love, a God who relents from sending calamity."

Jonah 4:2 NIV

Apart from the barbaric ways of the Ninevites, one of the primary reasons Jonah did not want to bring God's message to the people was that he did not believe they should receive God's mercy.

Have you found yourself deciding on God's behalf of who is deserving of His grace and mercy?

Though our brains are rooted in logic to make things easier each day, we must understand that God's love is anything but logical.

When we try to predict and carry out God's plan based on our limited understanding, we'll become disgruntled trying to make sense of where and how He extends His love.

But through our obedience, He works on our hearts, refines us, and brings glory to His name.

Considering we are all unworthy of God's grace and love, check your actions to discover any hindrances you might be creating.

READ

Grab your bible and look up the scripture to read the surrounding text.

EXAMINE

What is happening in this text?
What does it teach me about God?

APPLY

What does this mean for my life?

PRAY

The Great Liberator

DAY 22

"Arise quickly!" And his chains fell off his hands. Then the angel said to him, "Gird yourself and tie on your sandals"; and so he did. And he said to him, "Put on your garment and follow me.""

Acts 12:7-8 NKJV

How does a man go from denying Jesus outright three times after spending years with Him, to becoming the rock on which Jesus established the early church?

It's grace. Do you realize how messy the act of grace is? True grace is not straightforward; it doesn't always make sense. It's often very hard to do and takes much practice. However, we have plenty of examples as we've seen it on display throughout the Word of God.

It's a beautiful assurance to know that Jesus understands all our complexities like only a creator could.

This is why the Bible says let us then with confidence draw near to the throne of grace, that we may receive mercy and find grace to help in time of need (Hebrews 4:16).

Examine the beauty of God's grace—having seen every type of shame this world is able to cast on you, He alone can set you free and catapult you boldly into your purpose.

READ

Grab your bible and look up the scripture to read the surrounding text.

EXAMINE

What is happening in this text?
What does it teach me about God?

APPLY

What does this mean for my life?

PRAY

 **More Holy Spirit**

DAY 23

"For the flesh desires what is contrary to the Spirit, and the Spirit what is contrary to the flesh. They are in conflict with each other, so that you are not to do whatever you want."

Galatians 5:17 NIV

We all know the feeling. We understand the assignment, we know what's required, but when it comes to the test, we fail in our attempt or lack thereof.

Paul said it best "For I have the desire to do what is good, but I cannot carry it out. For I do not do the good I want to do, but the evil I do not want to do—this I keep on doing" (Romans 7:18-19 NIV).

God is still working on us, and He'll continue to as long as we occupy this world. But just like many of the individuals we've read about in the Bible, the struggles we'll have should not define us.

Rather, we should be known by our commitment to obey His words and the leading of the Holy Spirit. When we make way for the leading of the Holy Spirit, we create the necessary tension with our fleshly desires.

This is the tension needed to grow stronger in our walk, and it will happen as long as we apply God's wisdom.

READ

Grab your bible and look up the scripture to read the surrounding text.

EXAMINE

What is happening in this text?
What does it teach me about God?

APPLY

What does this mean for my life?

PRAY

# He's Still Here

DAY 24

"Soon the world will no longer see me, but you will see me. Since I live, you also will live."

John 14:19 NLT

Andy Mineo talks about a moment of anxiety during a flight. The overcast of the clouds and the turbulence during takeoff created a sense of fear.

Not until the plane elevated above the clouds did he remember that the sun was always there. Even though he could not see it, it didn't mean it was absent.

In our moments of doubt and anxiety, it's important to remember the promise

Jesus made to those who love Him.

He abides with us. Our circumstances, though they may get cloudy, do not mean He is absent.

Let's stand firm in our faith and expect that Jesus will reveal Himself in our times of need.

READ

Grab your bible and look up the scripture to read the surrounding text.

EXAMINE

What is happening in this text?
What does it teach me about God?

APPLY

What does this mean for my life?

PRAY

 # Bring Healing

DAY 25

"Some people make cutting remarks, but the words of the wise bring healing."

Proverbs 12:18 NLT

Have you noticed how a few words in a slight moment can pull you from joy?

I watched a friend boil in frustration for over five minutes from the words that a stranger expressed in less than five seconds.

Unbeknownst to this stranger, my friend had just lost her brother just a few days prior and was also nursing a painful hand injury. The stranger's slight comment on where my friend should leave her grocery cart after shopping felt vicious in that moment.

If the intent of that stranger's comment was to better serve their community in some way, it missed my friend. Each day we have countless opportunities to strengthen our communities. Often it's in comments expressed in less than five seconds, and other times it's not.

At the same time of that passing stranger's comment, without words, another stranger saw my friend's casted hand and decided to help return the cart.

As you've probably felt, words often have a deep impact on you.
Considering the passing comments and interactions we have, how do we make others feel after we've come and gone?

READ
Grab your bible and look up the scripture to read the surrounding text.

EXAMINE
What is happening in this text?
What does it teach me about God?

APPLY
What does this mean for my life?

PRAY

As iron sharpens iron, so one man sharpens another.

Proverbs 27:17

Weekly Reflection

 # He Knows the Way

DAY 26

"Search me, O God, and know my heart; test me and know my anxious thoughts. Point out anything in me that offends you, and lead me along the path of everlasting life."

Psalm 139:23-24 NLT

It's difficult for us to accurately assess ourselves. Some of us find it hard to identify any wrongdoings in our walk because we favorably compare ourselves with others.

Some of us find every issue with our existence, again comparing our journeys to others.

I've heard one pastor say it like this: comparison is the great thief of joy.

The best way for us to improve our walk is to allow our Creator, the One who knows everything about us, including our destination, to expose our hearts to His Word.

No one knows you like our God, not even you. Ask Him today to point your heart in the right direction, the direction that He has for you only.

READ

Grab your bible and look up the scripture to read the surrounding text.

EXAMINE

What is happening in this text?
What does it teach me about God?

APPLY

What does this mean for my life?

PRAY

 # Come to Know Him

DAY 27

"By his divine power, God has given us everything we need for living a godly life. We have received all of this by coming to know him, the one who called us to himself by means of his marvelous glory and excellence."

2 Peter 1:3 NLT

After passing year 8 in our marriage, I've realized that many of the disputes my wife and I had earlier in our marriage no longer happen. One reason for that is the intentionality we've had about having tough conversations–conversations that have forced us to really know and understand each other on a much deeper level.

Godly living requires a deeper-level relationship with God. Without deliberate seeking, without tough conversations about yourself and who He is to you, without listening, there is no relationship being built.

And without a true relationship, we cannot understand how to truly live a life that pleases Him, rather than the world.

This is why John says "But those who obey God's word truly show how completely they love him. That is how we know we are living in him. Those who say they live in God should live their lives as Jesus did" (1 John 2:5-6 NLT).

READ

Grab your bible and look up the scripture to read the surrounding text.

EXAMINE

What is happening in this text?
What does it teach me about God?

APPLY

What does this mean for my life?

PRAY

 **Greater Glory**

DAY 28

"For I consider that the sufferings of this present time are not worth comparing with the glory that is to be revealed to us."

Romans 8:18 ESV

Because of the experience of childbirth, women are probably closest in understanding what it means to suffer and then to have that pain be incomparably diminished by unspeakable joy.

And just like holding your child for the first time, it's hard to compare what you've never felt before. It's especially hard when you're faced with constant pain and turmoil over a period of time.

But we are assured that we will not be disappointed when God reveals His glory. Just as He did for Martha and Lazarus, and as He did for Moses. Our reference to what's possible is incomparable to the ways of God.

When it's hard to imagine overcoming, consider His faithfulness and remind yourself it is impossible to predict the grandeur of our Creator.

READ

Grab your bible and look up the scripture to read the surrounding text.

EXAMINE

What is happening in this text?
What does it teach me about God?

APPLY

What does this mean for my life?

PRAY

Surrounded by Your Glory

DAY 29

"For his invisible attributes, namely, his eternal power and divine nature, have been clearly perceived, ever since the creation of the world, in the things that have been made. So they are without excuse."

Romans 1:20 ESV

We are surrounded by parables. All of life points to the glory of God once we've been revealed to the light of Jesus.

The disciples may have found concepts of truth in observing seeds and a garden before their encounter with Jesus, but to see these concepts of truth and the kingdom of God revealed with Jesus changed our world and the understanding of our place in this world.

As you continue to dive into the Word of God, pray that He reveals His glory around you through everything He has made.

READ

Grab your bible and look up the scripture to read the surrounding text.

EXAMINE

What is happening in this text? What does it teach me about God?

APPLY

What does this mean for my life?

PRAY

📖 Our True Identity

DAY 30

"So all of us who have had that veil removed can see and reflect the glory of the Lord. And the Lord—who is the Spirit— makes us more and more like him as we are changed into his glorious image."

2 Corinthians 3:18 NLT

We were made in His image but have allowed the views of others to shape our identity.

Did you grow up in an environment where you were made to feel worthless or unloved?

Perhaps you were given labels based on other people's insecurities and limitations based on your parents' point of view.

Whatever label the world has placed on you, you do not have to buy into it.

The Bible shows us that once we believe in Jesus, the veil is removed, and we begin to know the truth. And the truth is you were made in His image, no matter what you've been labeled.

His glory resides in you because of Jesus. Whose truth are you accepting? The world's or God's?

READ

Grab your bible and look up the scripture to read the surrounding text.

EXAMINE

What is happening in this text?
What does it teach me about God?

APPLY

What does this mean for my life?

PRAY

Victory is won through many advisors.

Proverbs 24:6

Weekly Reflection

📖 Do Not Fear

DAY 31

"This is my commandment: Love each other in the same way I have loved you. There is no greater love than to lay down one's life for one's friends."

John 15:12-13 NLT

Have you, like many of us, become calloused to those who are hurting among us?

MLK once said that "there can be no deep disappointment where there is not deep love."

One of the reasons why Jesus warns of the trouble we'll have in this world is due to the disappointment we will face. We have been commanded to love, therefore we will experience disappointment often for and from those we love and care for.

Don't let the fear of disappointment deter you from obeying Jesus's commands. That sacrificial love He displayed is not only a force for great change in our world, it is how we're identified as followers of Christ.

READ

Grab your bible and look up the scripture to read the surrounding text.

EXAMINE

What is happening in this text?
What does it teach me about God?

APPLY

What does this mean for my life?

PRAY

I've Got Something to Share

DAY 32

"We are confident that as you share in our sufferings, you will also share in the comfort God gives us."

2 Corinthians 1:7 NLT

The early church relied heavily on one another. It was common to see the sharing of goods for the body to sustain.

Another form of sharing we saw was that of grief and burden. Paul both wrote and received letters on the sufferings that followers of Christ were dealing with.

What's interesting is that the sharing of these letters was not merely to gain pity on one's situation but to invite the promise of comfort that only other believers could resonate with. Paul writes that it is good for others to be aware of the sufferings, for they had to rely only on God who was able to deliver them as He had done before, giving hope even in their moments of deepest despair.

That same hope and testimony of deliverance are abundantly available to those who rely on Jesus.

Take inventory of the relationships God has given you. Do they know the comfort of your God?

READ

Grab your bible and look up the scripture to read the surrounding text.

EXAMINE

What is happening in this text?
What does it teach me about God?

APPLY

What does this mean for my life?

PRAY

 # Hold on to This

DAY 33

"Do not conform to the pattern of this world, but be transformed by the renewing of your mind. Then you will be able to test and approve what God's will is—his good, pleasing and perfect will."

Romans 12:2 NIV

Every time we move to a new home, I'm reminded of how much stuff we as people can quickly accumulate over short periods of time. It is said that the average American home has 300,000 items–300,000!

It's easy to notice all the physical baggage we collect over time, but it's a bit harder to identify the mental load we're also accumulating throughout our days.

For this reason alone, it's important for us to seek God's renewal daily. Knowing what to keep and what to throw away as it pertains to you can only be properly determined by the One who truly knows you.

READ

Grab your bible and look up the scripture to read the surrounding text.

EXAMINE

What is happening in this text? What does it teach me about God?

APPLY

What does this mean for my life?

PRAY

📖 A Heavenly Focus

DAY 34

"That is why we never give up. Though our bodies are dying, our spirits are being renewed every day. For our present troubles are small and won't last very long. Yet they produce for us a glory that vastly outweighs them and will last forever!"

2 Corinthians 4:16–17 NLT

To the Corinthians, Paul writes that our bodies are like clay jars containing this great light and treasure.

Though there is a physical limitation to our bodies in this world, we carry a light that has eternal power. As more people see this light given to us by Jesus, our spirit can rejoice knowing the eternal reward ahead even though we may face physical suffering.

Consider our time here in this world compared to eternity, or one grain of sand compared to the vastness of the Saharan desert. An eternal perspective is essential as a believer and keeps our spirits renewed through hardship.

Don't give up today. Let your light shine, and rejoice because your Lord is being glorified through your obedience.

READ
Grab your bible and look up the scripture to read the surrounding text.

EXAMINE
What is happening in this text?
What does it teach me about God?

APPLY
What does this mean for my life?

PRAY

 # Strong Fellowship

DAY 35

"Let us think of ways to motivate one another to acts of love and good works. And let us not neglect our meeting together, as some people do, but encourage one another, especially now that the day of his return is drawing near."

Hebrews 10:24-25 NLT

An essential in Christian living is true Christian fellowship. Men often find it difficult to develop meaningful relationships that will go beyond surface interactions to strengthen one another's faith.

Examine closely and notice how the men of God throughout scripture remained in the presence of other godly men to accomplish their purpose.

Without David's men of Valor, Gideon's 300, Paul's companions, could these individuals carry the enormous weight they encountered?

These relationships rarely happen naturally; they are to be cultivated through time, intentional conversations, and the invitation of God's presence in your relationship.

If you have this type of relationship, send your gratitude to these men. If not, start with prayer asking God to bless you with such relationships.

READ

Grab your bible and look up the scripture to read the surrounding text.

EXAMINE

What is happening in this text?
What does it teach me about God?

APPLY

What does this mean for my life?

PRAY

Pursue
righteousness

1 Timothy 6:11

Weekly Reflection

Remember What He Has Done

DAY 36

"Let all that I am praise the LORD; may I never forget the good things he does for me."

Psalm 103:2 NLT

Sometimes we have to pause and reflect to understand all the ways God is working in our lives.

Our confidence grows from acknowledging God's faithfulness. Our busyness, scattered thoughts, and doubts aren't stopping Him from being who He is; they only limit us from recognizing all that He is.

Because He is faithful and always true, it is always the right time to praise our God, for He never stops being Himself, we just sometimes fail to recognize who He is.

Have you made it a habit to remember all the good things God has done for you?

READ

Grab your bible and look up the scripture to read the surrounding text.

EXAMINE

What is happening in this text?
What does it teach me about God?

APPLY

What does this mean for my life?

PRAY

📖 All for His Glory

DAY 37

"So whether you eat or drink, or whatever you do, do it all for the glory of God."

1 Corinthians 10:31 NLT

There's a good reason why self-help books and coaches all over the world encourage people to do the work with the end in mind, the why behind it all.

Why are you doing this? What does it lead to? These are important questions. Merely living by the moment suggests that there's no purpose behind our decisions.

As followers of Christ, our purpose is to glorify God. With everything He has given us, we must point people to Him. We do not walk aimlessly; no, we each have a purpose, and we must be intentional and disciplined in order to see God's purpose manifested in our lives.

How your purpose is carried out is between you and God, revealed to you through humility and His wisdom, but it all points back to your Creator.

READ

Grab your bible and look up the scripture to read the surrounding text.

EXAMINE

What is happening in this text?
What does it teach me about God?

APPLY

What does this mean for my life?

PRAY

Come Together

DAY 38

"The glory that you have given me I have given to them, that they may be one even as we are one, I in them and you in me, that they may become perfectly one, so that the world may know that you sent me and loved them even as you loved me."

John 17: 22-23 ESV

The relationship that Jesus has with the Father is the relationship that He wishes to emulate with us. God the Father and Jesus displayed a love that is sacrificial, and actionable.

This time that we're living in where believers are divided amongst one another isn't foreign. We can see the results from the variety in denominations to the opinions we blast on social media.

Jesus knew this would happen, and He prayed for us. His prayer for oneness among believers was essential. We help to unify others in our world by sharing the truth of the Gospel.

The truth, God's Word according to Jesus, would not only set us free from the world's bondage, but it would unite us.

READ
Grab your bible and look up the scripture to read the surrounding text.

EXAMINE
What is happening in this text?
What does it teach me about God?

APPLY
What does this mean for my life?

PRAY

 Know the Strategies

DAY 39

"Next the devil took him to the peak of a very high mountain and showed him all the kingdoms of the world and their glory."

Matthew 4:8 NLT

It is important for us to be aware of the strategies of the devil. Many of his strategies are the same, recycled for our present time, but we often perish due to a lack of knowledge of God's Word.

Satan has the ability to manipulate scripture through many outlets in our world today. He's also very good at showing us flashes of what is glorified here on earth.

Leaning on God's strength and Word, Jesus gives us hope and a framework for the strategies that the devil will bring to us.

How can you apply God's strength and Word to the deceptions that you're facing today?

READ
Grab your bible and look up the scripture to read the surrounding text.

EXAMINE
What is happening in this text?
What does it teach me about God?

APPLY
What does this mean for my life?

PRAY

He Knows Your Load

DAY 40

"In the morning you will see the glory of the LORD, because he has heard your complaints, which are against him, not against us. What have we done that you should complain about us?"

Exodus 16:7 NLT

I've heard the joke several times from different pastors that if it had not been for people, they'd be great pastors.

Pastoring, like most leadership positions, is primarily about people–and people are difficult.

Consensus is hard enough to get between two persons, much less among many. This passage of scripture depicting Moses' qualms with the Israelite people validates the difficulty of spiritual leadership.

But just as Moses expresses, it's important to acknowledge that when you as a leader are close to the heart of God and making decisions based on that relationship, the quarrels aren't your burden to bear.

Lean on God in these times of frustration, for He seeks to lighten your load.

READ

Grab your bible and look up the scripture to read the surrounding text.

EXAMINE

What is happening in this text?
What does it teach me about God?

APPLY

What does this mean for my life?

PRAY

The testing of your faith produces perseverence.

James 1:3

Weekly Reflection

ABOUT THE AUTHOR- JERMAINE MALCOLM

Being an immigrant from Jamaica and a former college football player, I'm fascinated by the journeys we take as individuals that reveal our purpose. The common thread in my career has been bridging the gaps for those who need it the most, as a Director of the Boys and Girls Club, a Community Engagement Consultant for the My Brother's Keeper Initiative, and in my role for one of the nation's first tech apprenticeships. My story is about seeing further by standing on the shoulders of giants, and gladly teaching what I am learning.

—

From an early age, I knew I wanted to be like one person in my life—my grandmother. Her example of faithfulness through my formative years in Jamaica gave me the confidence to believe in the hope of Jesus.

My work to bridge the gaps in our communities through mentorship and relevant resources is a testament to the faithfulness of my grandmother and other giants in my life who have allowed me to see further.

—

Just a few years ago, I realized the common thread throughout my career and ministry. That is to bridge skills and opportunity gaps for those that need it most through relevant mentorship and resources.

My hope is for individuals to move from one place to the next destination with excitement and hope for the future.

Made in United States
Orlando, FL
21 November 2023

39268133R00057